Mastering Real Estate

A Guide To Comprehensive Estate Management

By

Bill P. Beck

TABLE OF CONTENTS

INTRODUCTION

Real estate management stands as a dynamic and crucial discipline within the larger spectrum of property and asset administration. This opening chapter seeks to offer readers a clear grasp of the book's objective, the relevance of estate management, and an overall overview of the issues to be discussed.

Purpose of the Book

In digging into the goal of this book, our major objective is to provide both rookie and seasoned experts in the real estate sector with a complete guide to successful estate management. Whether you are a property owner, investor, or aspiring real estate professional, the insights within these pages seek to boost your understanding and expertise in navigating the vast environment of property management.

Overview of Estate Management

To engage in a meaningful examination of estate administration, it is necessary to appreciate the broad extent and diverse character of this topic.

This section gives an overview of the fundamental ideas, duties, and responsibilities connected with good estate administration. From legal issues to strategic planning, readers will receive useful insights into the numerous components that contribute to successful property management.

As we journey through the chapters that follow, each section is thoughtfully prepared to give practical direction, theoretical foundations, and real-world experiences.

The trip begins with developing a firm foundation in the principles of estate administration and develops towards an investigation of legal frameworks, property kinds, valuation methodologies, development plans, and the subtleties of property marketing and management.

By the end of this book, readers will not only possess a complete grasp of estate management but will also be well-equipped to apply this knowledge in diverse real-world circumstances.

Let's go on this instructive voyage into the world of estate management, where each chapter serves as a stepping stone towards mastery and perfection in the area of real estate.

CHAPTER ONE

Fundamentals of Estate Management

Through the planned and all-encompassing administration of a variety of real estate holdings, estate management ensures that these properties are utilized to their full potential, that they are sustainable, and that their value is increased. Due to the fact that the global scene is always shifting, the job of estate management has become increasingly important.

This role requires a comprehensive awareness of the legal, financial, and operational elements of the situation.

At its foundation, estate management comprises the skilled control of varied property portfolios, ranging from residential and commercial real estate to industrial and agricultural assets. Estate managers that are successful negotiate a complicated landscape of rules, market forces, and stakeholder interests in order to achieve the overriding aim of maximizing the potential of any property that falls under their jurisdiction.

This multidimensional field involves a wide range of essential components, such as the administration of leases, the maintenance of facilities, the management of risks, and the planning of strategic actions. In their capacity as guardians of both the actual assets and the intangible values connected with real estate, estate managers are tasked with striking a balance between short-term goals and long-term sustainability. They are responsible for cultivating settings that are able to flourish despite the fluctuations in the economy and the changes in society.

Furthermore, it is very necessary for estate managers to have a comprehensive awareness of the legal frameworks that regulate real property. The ability to navigate the legal landscape assures not only the preservation of property rights but also the appropriate and ethical management of real estate assets. This includes ensuring compliance with environmental standards and zoning restrictions within the legal system.

The ability to handle budgets, anticipate market trends, and maximize revenue sources is another essential component of estate administration. Professionals in this field are required to have a strong grasp of financial matters. The adoption of value-enhancing initiatives and sustainable development practices is made possible by a strategic financial strategy, which not only protects the estate's financial health but also makes it possible to apply these activities.

It is apparent that success in this profession demands a complete skill set that goes beyond standard property management.

It needs a strategic vision, flexibility to change, and a commitment to ethical practices that contribute not just to the financial prosperity of property owners but also to the well-being of the communities within which these estates live. In the following examination, we will go further into each essential feature, uncovering the complexities that distinguish this dynamic and changing profession.

Definition and Scope

Estate management is a comprehensive profession that covers the strategic control, administration, and optimization of numerous real estates. At its heart, it extends beyond the conventional idea of property management, encompassing a larger range of duties to enhance the value, usefulness, and sustainability of real estate assets.

Estate management may be described as the systematic and strategic administration of real property, comprising a range of operations aimed at maximizing its potential worth, maintaining legal compliance, and supporting sustainable growth. This multidimensional field demands a profound grasp of property law, finance, facilities management, and market dynamics.

Scope
Property Valuation:

Objective: Determine the true market value of a property.

Scope: Estate managers apply several valuation methodologies to determine the worth of real estate, considering aspects such as location, market trends, and property condition. Accurate appraisals are vital for making educated decisions regarding investment, development, or sale.

Legal Compliance and Risk Management:

Objective: Ensure conformity to legal frameworks and reduce any hazards.

Scope: Estate managers traverse complicated legal environments, addressing issues relating to zoning restrictions, land use, environmental compliance, and property rights. By maintaining aware of legal requirements, they preserve the interests of property owners and stakeholders.

Lease Administration:

Objective: Effectively handle lease agreements to optimize income and tenant relationships.

Scope: Estate managers oversee the negotiation, writing, and enforcement of lease agreements. This involves rent collection, lease renewals, and handling tenant problems. Efficient lease administration helps to a constant cash stream and tenant satisfaction.

Financial Management:

Objective: Optimize financial performance and budgeting for real estate assets.

Scope: Estate managers establish and execute budgets, conduct financial assessments, and implement strategies to optimize returns on investment.

Financial management entails projecting market trends, monitoring operating expenses, and making educated decisions to maximize asset value.

Facility Maintenance and Development:

Objective: Ensure the physical integrity and improvement of real estate assets.

Scope: Estate managers oversee the upkeep, refurbishment, and development of properties. This involves resolving structural flaws, employing sustainable practices, and using technological improvements to increase overall efficiency and functioning.

Stakeholder Relations:

Objective: Foster positive connections with property owners, tenants, and the community.

Scope: Estate managers operate as liaisons between property owners and stakeholders. Effective communication and community participation contribute to a favorable image, tenant retention, and the overall success of the estate.

Strategic Planning:

Objective: Develop and implement long-term plans for estate growth and sustainability.

Scope: Estate managers design strategic plans that coincide with the interests of property owners. This comprises market analysis, finding growth prospects, and adjusting to altering economic and sociological trends.

Importance of Effective Management

Effective management serves as the cornerstone of success in estate management, playing a crucial role in increasing the value, efficiency, and sustainability of real estate assets. In the evolving environment of property administration, the value of skilled management cannot be emphasized, as it directly effects the financial performance, tenant happiness, and overall profitability of a real estate portfolio.

Optimizing Financial Performance

Strategic Decision-Making: Effective management entails making educated decisions to optimize the financial performance of real estate assets. This involves budgeting, financial forecasting, and adopting techniques that optimize returns on investment.

Risk Mitigation: Proficient estate managers detect and reduce financial risks, ensuring that the estate remains robust in the face of economic swings, market uncertainty, and unanticipated problems.

Enhancing Property Value

Strategic Planning: A fundamental part of good estate management is strategic planning. Managers design and implement long-term plans that increase the value of assets. This may encompass restorations, sustainable development techniques, and remaining ahead of market developments to capitalize on value-adding possibilities.

Property Maintenance: Timely and proactive maintenance is vital for sustaining the physical integrity of real estate assets. Effective management ensures that properties are well-maintained, contributing to their durability and general market appeal.

Tenant Satisfaction and Retention

Lease Administration: Proficient estate managers thrive in lease administration, handling tenant problems, and maintaining excellent landlord-tenant relationships. This not only increases tenant contentment but also adds to tenant retention, decreasing vacancy rates and assuring a constant income stream.

Community Engagement: Effective management extends beyond individual properties to community engagement.

Managers who appreciate the value of developing excellent ties with the community contribute to a favorable image for the estate, attracting great tenants and stakeholders.

Legal Compliance and Ethical Practices

Navigating Legal Complexities: Estate managers competent in legal concerns guarantee that real estate assets conform with zoning restrictions, environmental standards, and other legal obligations. This not only protects the interests of property owners but also supports ethical practices in property management.

Ethical Decision-Making: Upholding ethical norms is crucial in estate management.

Effective managers stress openness, justice, and accountability, developing confidence with property owners, renters, and stakeholders.

Adapting to Technological Advancements

Incorporating Technology: The contemporary estate manager realizes the relevance of technology in simplifying processes and boosting efficiency. Integration of property management software, data analytics, and smart building technology enhances decision-making processes, saves operating costs, and assures a competitive advantage in the market.

Strategic Relationship Building

Stakeholder Relations: Effective estate managers work as strategic liaisons between property owners, renters, and other stakeholders. Cultivating healthy connections via clear communication, attentiveness, and a dedication to addressing stakeholder requirements is vital for long-term success.

CHAPTER TWO

Legal Framework and Contracts

In the convoluted area of real estate management, a comprehensive awareness of the legal landscape is vital. This chapter dives into the legal framework controlling real estate transactions, property ownership, and the contractual subtleties that characterize these relationships.

Property Laws and Regulations

In the world of estate administration, a sophisticated awareness of property laws and regulations is vital.

These legal frameworks serve as the cornerstone, giving the structure and principles that regulate the ownership, use, and administration of real estate assets. Estate managers, serving as custodians of these assets, must traverse a complicated regulatory framework to assure compliance, safeguard the interests of property owners, and develop ethical standards in the administration of real estates.

1. **Property Ownership and Transfers**

Title Deeds and Conveyance: Understanding the complexity of property ownership begins with a comprehension of title deeds and the conveyance procedure.

Estate managers need to confirm the integrity of property titles, validating the legal ownership of assets and arranging legitimate transfers as necessary.

Easements and Encumbrances: Estate managers must be well-versed in easements and encumbrances, as these legal principles can effect property usage and development. Being aware of any limits or allowances ensures that management choices fit with legal responsibilities.

2. **Zoning Regulations and Land Use**

Zoning Codes: Local zoning rules limit the legal uses of property in specified localities. Estate managers need to interpret zoning rules to ensure that properties comply with assigned land use categories, eliminating potential legal difficulties and improving property value.

Land Use Planning: Understanding land use planning is vital for estate managers since it includes managing property development in compliance with municipal plans. Compliance with these plans not only assures legality but also contributes to sustainable and harmonious urban or rural development.

3. **Lease Agreements and Tenancy Laws**

Lease Contract Compliance: Effective lease management involves a full awareness of tenancy regulations. Estate managers must develop, negotiate, and enforce lease agreements in line with existing rules, ensuring the interests of both landlords and renters.

Tenant Rights and obligations: Staying knowledgeable about tenant rights and obligations is vital for estate managers. This understanding assists in addressing tenant issues, preventing conflicts, and building a positive and legally sound landlord-tenant relationship.

4. **Environmental Regulations**

Environmental effect Assessments (EIA): Estate managers should be aware of environmental rules that effect property development. Conducting EIAs when necessary assures compliance with environmental regulations, mitigates hazards, and encourages sustainable practices.

Waste Management and Pollution Control: Adhering to waste management and pollution control standards is vital for real estate assets.

Estate managers play a significant role in establishing procedures that reduce environmental effect and maintain compliance with regulatory regulations.

5. Fair Housing Laws

Anti-Discrimination Legislation: Estate managers must be well-versed in fair housing legislation to prevent discrimination in housing operations. Knowledge of protected groups, reasonable accommodation criteria, and accessible design standards is crucial for legal and ethical property management.

6. Eviction Procedures and Legal Remedies

Legal Process Knowledge: In circumstances when eviction becomes required, estate managers must be knowledgeable with legal eviction procedures. Understanding the legal remedies available and following due procedure guarantees that the eviction is carried out within the confines of the law.

7. Ethical Considerations

Transparency and Accountability: While not exactly legal, ethical issues are fundamental to estate administration.

Estate managers must respect values of openness, fairness, and accountability, not just to comply with legal criteria but also to promote confidence among property owners, renters, and other stakeholders.

Real Estate Contracts

Real estate contracts provide the cornerstone of transactions within the field of estate management, establishing the rights, liabilities, and expectations of parties engaged in the ownership, use, and administration of real property. These legally enforceable agreements serve as vital instruments for effective estate management, altering the dynamics of interactions between property owners, tenants, and other stakeholders.

A detailed awareness of the complexity of real estate contracts is crucial for estate managers to negotiate the complexities of the sector and maintain the seamless operating of property portfolios.

1. **Types of Real Estate Contracts**

Purchase and Sale Agreements: These contracts detail the terms and conditions regulating the transfer of ownership between a buyer and a seller. Estate managers engage in the negotiation and drafting of these agreements, providing clarity on the purchase price, closing dates, and any contingencies that may emerge.

Lease Agreements: Fundamental in the rental component of estate management, lease agreements establish the terms under which a tenant occupies a property. Estate managers play a crucial role in designing leases, addressing concerns such as rent levels, lease term, maintenance responsibilities, and tenant requirements.

Property Management Agreements: When property owners employ the services of estate managers, a property management agreement is formed. This contract delineates the scope of obligations, remuneration arrangements, and the duration of the management agreement.

Construction Contracts: In circumstances when development or rehabilitation projects are performed, construction contracts come into play. Estate managers must oversee the negotiation and implementation of these agreements, ensuring that building activities fit with the property owner's objectives.

2. Key Components of Real Estate Contracts

Identification of Parties: Contracts expressly identify the parties involved, including the buyer, seller, landlord, renter, and any other important stakeholders. Clear identification is vital for legal clarity and enforcement.

Property Description: Accurate and accurate descriptions of the property in question are vital. This comprises not just the actual address but also data regarding borders, easements, and other significant qualities impacting the property.

Terms and Conditions: Real estate contracts specify the terms and conditions agreed upon by the parties. These may contain the purchase price, payment schedules, leasing terms, maintenance duties, and any contingencies that need to be addressed.

Legal Considerations: Contracts involve legal components like as compliance with zoning restrictions, environmental standards, and other legal obligations.

Estate managers verify that contracts fit with current rules and regulations.

3. Contract Negotiation and Drafting

Bargaining abilities: Estate managers must exhibit great bargaining abilities to get advantageous conditions for their clients. Whether negotiating lease terms, purchase pricing, or management fees, successful negotiation adds to the success of the estate.

Clarity in Drafting: Real estate contracts necessitate clarity in language and terminology.

Estate managers, frequently working in tandem with legal specialists, must write contracts that appropriately reflect the interests of the parties involved, eliminating ambiguity and potential disagreements.

4. **Compliance and Enforceability**

Legal Compliance: Estate managers are responsible for ensuring that contracts conform to all applicable laws and regulations. This involves confirming that the provisions of the contract correspond with local zoning regulations, construction codes, and other legal requirements.

Enforceability: Contracts must be constructed to be legally enforceable. Estate managers endeavor to construct agreements that stand up to legal examination and give a framework for resolution in the case of conflicts.

5. **Risk Management**

Contingency Planning: Real estate contracts sometimes include contingency clauses to manage unanticipated occurrences. Estate managers must carefully analyze and plan for potential hazards, adopting procedures that protect the interests of their customers.

Dispute settlement: Contracts often contain mechanisms for dispute settlement, including mediation, arbitration, or legal action. Estate managers have a role in easing settlement procedures and limiting the impact of conflicts on property management.

6. Evolving Trends and Technologies

Digital Contracts: With the introduction of technology, the estate management sector is experiencing a trend towards digital contracts. Estate managers are increasingly adopting electronic signatures, secure online platforms, and block chain technology to increase the efficiency and security of contract execution.

Smart Contracts: The introduction of smart contracts, enabled by block chain technology, provides a unique method to automating and self-executing contractual agreements. While still in the early stages of implementation, smart contracts offer the potential to simplify certain parts of estate management contracts.

CHAPTER THREE
Valuation and Development

In the changing world of real estate, recognizing the value of assets and the strategic planning necessary for development are key components of efficient estate management. This chapter discusses the nuances of property valuation methodologies and the important ingredients of successful property development.

Property Valuation Methods

Property valuation is a key part of real estate management, since it entails assessing the monetary worth of a property. Accurate valuation is vital for different objectives, such as purchasing and selling, financing, insurance, taxation, and investment analysis. There are various approaches applied in property valuation, each having its own strengths and limits. Mastering real estate management demands a full comprehension of these strategies to make educated judgments. Here, we'll study several major property valuation methods:

1. **Market Comparison Approach**

- Overview: This strategy focuses on comparing the subject property to similar properties that have recently been sold in the market.

- Strengths: Straightforward and intuitive. It evaluates the market demand and supply for similar assets.

- Limitations: Highly dependent on the availability of comparable sales data. Adjustments for variations between attributes may be subjective.

2. **Income Capitalization Approach**

- Overview: Particularly significant for income-generating properties, this technique determines the property's worth based on its earning potential.

- Strengths: Directly connects property worth to its income-earning capability. Commonly used for commercial real estate.

- Limitations: Accuracy depends on precise income and cost estimates. Market circumstances might fluctuate, influencing revenue sources.

3. **Cost Approach**

- Overview: Evaluates the cost of replacing or replicating the property, deducting depreciation.

- Strengths: Useful for unique or specialized features. Provides a foundation for minimal property value.

- Limitations: Ignores market dynamics and current property status. Depreciation estimate might be subjective.

4. **Residual Valuation**

- Overview: Often utilized in property development, it determines the worth of the developed property by deducting development expenses from the predicted future value.

- Strengths: Useful for determining the viability of development initiatives.

- Limitations: Requires correct prediction of future property value and construction expenditures.

5. **Discounted Cash Flow (DCF) Analysis**

- Overview: Commonly used for investment properties, DCF calculates the present value of future cash flows.

- Strengths: Incorporates the time worth of money. Useful for long-term investment analysis.

- Limitations: Relies largely on precise cash flow predictions and discount rate assumptions.

6. **Automated Valuation Models (AVMs)**

- Overview: Utilizes computer algorithms to examine data and generate property assessments.

- Strengths: Provides speedy and cost-effective appraisals. It can process big datasets.

- Limitations: Accuracy relies on the quality of data input. It may lack the human judgment aspect.

Mastering property valuation in real estate management includes a sophisticated grasp of these approaches and the ability to use them correctly based on the property type, market circumstances, and the objective of the value. It also demands being current on market trends, legislation, and economic issues that might affect property prices.

Successful real estate managers employ a combination of these valuation methodologies, recognizing their strengths and limits, to arrive at a well-informed and defensible property value.

Planning and Feasibility Studies

Planning and feasibility studies are key components in understanding real estate management, playing a crucial role in assuring the success of a real estate project. These methods entail a complete examination and evaluation of many criteria to determine the profitability, sustainability, and possible success of a real estate enterprise.

Here's a high-quality review of Planning and Feasibility Studies in understanding real estate management:

Strategic Vision and Goal Alignment:

Planning establishes the foundation for each successful real estate endeavor. It entails defining a strategic vision and integrating project goals with the wider objectives of the real estate portfolio or company.

Feasibility studies, in turn, dig into the feasibility of accomplishing these aims, exploring potential challenges and possibilities.

Market Analysis:

A comprehensive grasp of the market is vital. Planning comprises a complete market study, detecting trends, demand-supply dynamics, and competitive landscapes.

Feasibility studies analyze the market's receptiveness to the proposed project, establishing if there is a sustained demand and potential for lucrative outcomes.

Financial Viability:

One of the key topics of feasibility studies is financial analysis. This comprises analyzing the cost of development, predicted revenues, and potential return on investment.

Planning ensures that financial goals are feasible and connected with the organization's financial plan, giving a sound financial framework for the feasibility study.

Risk Assessment and Mitigation:

Both planning and feasibility studies require a detailed risk assessment. Identifying possible obstacles and uncertainties is key for successful risk management.

Feasibility studies go a step further by providing risk mitigation techniques, allowing stakeholders to make educated decisions based on a thorough understanding of potential obstacles.

Regulatory Compliance:

Planning involves an assessment of regulatory requirements, zoning regulations, and other legal factors. Ensuring compliance is vital for the effective implementation of a real estate project.

Feasibility studies analyze the possible impact of regulatory requirements on the project, delivering insights into potential delays or adjustments needed to fulfill legal standards.

Environmental Impact and Sustainability:

A complete planning approach incorporates environmental effect and sustainability.

This entails examining the ecological footprint of the project and developing solutions to reduce negative consequences.

Feasibility studies further analyze the possibility of applying sustainable practices, examining their influence on project costs and long-term benefits.

Stakeholder Engagement:

Planning entails identifying and interacting with important stakeholders, understanding their expectations, and aligning project goals with their requirements.

Feasibility studies examine stakeholder satisfaction, ensuring that the project not only satisfies financial criteria but also matches with the larger expectations of the community and investors.

Flexibility and Adaptability:

Planning should provide for flexibility in response to changing market conditions or unanticipated problems.

Feasibility studies involve scenarios and sensitivity analysis, ensuring that the project stays adaptive and robust in the face of changing economic, social, or environmental conditions.

CHAPTER FOUR

Property Management and Marketing

Property Management

Property management is the full control and administration of real estate assets on behalf of property owners. It covers many activities such as property upkeep, tenant interactions, rent collecting, budgeting, and assuring compliance with local rules. Effective property management attempts to maximize the property's worth while maintaining a positive and productive relationship between landlords and renters.

Successful property managers excel in communication, organization, financial management, and legal understanding.

Marketing in Real Estate Management

Marketing in real estate management comprises advertising and presenting properties to attract new renters or purchasers. It comprises a deliberate approach to presenting properties in the best light, leveraging multiple marketing channels such as internet platforms, social media, and conventional means. Effective real estate marketing entails recognizing target consumers, stressing unique selling qualities, and employing technology to boost exposure.

An effective marketing plan not only speeds property leasing or sales but also adds to developing a strong brand presence in the real estate industry.

Tenant Relations and Lease Management

Certainly! Managing tenant relations and lease agreements is a critical component of understanding real estate management. This requires creating and maintaining strong connections with renters while assuring the proper administration of lease agreements.

Here are crucial factors to consider for high-quality tenant interactions and lease management:

Communication Skills:

Effective communication is vital in answering tenant complaints, explaining lease conditions, and creating a healthy landlord-tenant relationship.

Regularly informing renters on property-related concerns, regulatory changes, and forthcoming events leads to openness and confidence.

Responsive Maintenance and Repairs:

Timely attention to maintenance requests promotes tenant satisfaction. Implementing a proactive maintenance approach helps avert concerns, decreasing interruptions and enhancing overall property value.

Clear Lease Agreements:

Well-drafted, transparent leasing agreements are crucial for preventing misunderstandings and legal difficulties. Clear conditions about rent, obligations, and maintenance requirements should be written fully.

Tenant Retention Strategies:

Implementing strategies to increase tenant loyalty helps lower turnover expenses. This may involve providing exceptional customer service, giving incentives for lease renewals, and immediately addressing issues.

Legal Compliance:

Staying current on local and national rental rules is vital. Adhering to legal standards in lease agreements benefits both landlords and renters, preventing disagreements and potential legal concerns.

Technology Integration:

Utilizing property management software may expedite lease administration, rent collecting, and maintenance requests. Automation may boost efficiency and minimize the chance of mistakes.

Proactive Conflict Resolution:

Addressing disagreements immediately and properly is vital for sustaining a pleasant atmosphere. Developing excellent conflict resolution skills helps prevent possible conflicts and contribute to a harmonious community.

Financial Management

Efficient financial management involves precise rent collecting, budgeting, and financial reporting. Regularly assessing the financial condition of the property assures sustainability and profitability.

Community Building:

Fostering a feeling of community can lead to happy renters. Organizing activities, establishing shared areas, and fostering social interactions contribute to a pleasant living environment.

Regular Property Inspections:

Periodic inspections help discover possible concerns before they worsen.

This proactive approach adds to the general maintenance and upkeep of the property.

Marketing Strategies for Real Estate

Creating successful marketing tactics is vital in the real estate sector, and mastering real estate management entails understanding and executing plans that correspond with the current market trends. Here are some high-quality, real-time marketing methods for real estate:

Digital Presence and SEO

Establish a powerful internet presence with a quality website.

Optimize the website for search engines (SEO) to boost exposure.

Utilize social media networks to market properties and communicate with potential clients.

Virtual Tours with 3D Imaging

Implement virtual tours and 3D imaging for property listings to give a thorough perspective for potential purchasers.

Leverage sophisticated technology like augmented reality (AR) for an immersive experience.

Content Marketing

Create high-quality material like as blog articles, videos, and info graphics to exhibit industry knowledge.

Address common real estate problems, market trends, and give relevant insights to attract and maintain a target audience.

Email Marketing

Build and maintain a comprehensive email list.

Send out frequent emails with property updates, market trends, and unique offers to keep clients interested.

Targeted Advertising

Utilize paid advertising on sites like Google Ads and social media to target certain groups.

Implement retargeting methods to re-engage visitors who have showed interest in your listings.

Collaborations & Partnerships

Form collaborations with local companies, influencers, or other real estate professionals to extend your network.

Cross promote services and listings to reach a bigger audience.

Client Testimonials and Reviews

Showcase favorable client testimonials and reviews on your website and marketing materials.

Encourage happy clients to share their experiences on internet review networks.

Community Involvement

Participate at local events and fund community activities to develop trust and confidence.

Establish yourself as a dependable and engaged member of the community.

Data Analytics

Use data analytics tools to track and assess the effectiveness of your marketing activities.

Adjust tactics depending on the insights acquired to optimize for better results.

Personal Branding

Develop a strong personal brand as a real estate agent.

Utilize personal branding in your marketing materials and online presence to generate trust and awareness.

CHAPTER FIVE

Investment Strategies and Emerging Trends

In the area of real estate management, a detailed grasp of investment techniques is vital for navigating the changing terrain. Diversification stands out as a cornerstone idea, advocating for the prudent dispersion of assets across varied property kinds and geographical areas. This technique acts as a risk reduction tool, guaranteeing a balanced portfolio capable of weathering market swings while optimizing total returns.

Data-driven decision-making has emerged as a pillar in modern real estate investment. Leveraging modern analytics, investors obtain insights into developing trends, market circumstances, and possible opportunities. This analytical acumen helps stakeholders to make educated choices, aligning investments with current market dynamics and boosting the likelihood of success.

Integration of technology is crucial in understanding real estate management. Pro tech solutions not only improve property management procedures but also boost tenant involvement.

Staying alert to technology changes positions investors to remain competitive and benefit on efficiency improvements within the sector.

Sustainable investment has gained significance as environmental issues take center stage. Investors are increasingly factoring in environmental, social, and governance (ESG) factors, aligning their portfolios with sustainability goals. This method not only addresses the increased demand for eco-friendly properties but also positions investors advantageously in a market that rewards responsible activities.

On the operational level, a focus on value-add possibilities remains an effective strategy. Identifying assets with latent potential for renovation or redevelopment helps investors to strategically boost value. This might comprise targeted upgrades, repositioning within the market, or inventive makeovers that increase a property's desirability.

In parallel with investment strategies, identifying new trends is crucial for real estate management success. Remote property management has become a focus area, with technology permitting virtual property tours, online leasing, and remote monitoring.

This trend responds to the increasing interests and wants of a digitally aware tenant population.

The merging of living and working areas marks another noteworthy development. With the advent of flexible work arrangements, including co-living and co-working spaces into real estate portfolios answers the desire for versatile, multipurpose settings.

Wellness factors are increasingly impacting real estate selections. Properties providing green areas, fitness amenities, and health-focused designs appeal to a demographic placing a premium on holistic well-being.

This tendency reflects a larger cultural shift towards healthier living settings.

Addressing the affordable housing crisis is a critical trend needing new solutions. Real estate management solutions that focus on cost-effective housing alternatives react to societal requirements while offering potential for sustainable, socially responsible investments.

Lastly, keeping adaptive in adjusting to regulatory changes is crucial. Real estate investors must be watchful regarding increasing regulations, spanning zoning rules, rent restrictions, and environmental standards.

Proactively managing this regulatory terrain assures long-term sustainability and compliance.

Real Estate Investment Strategies

Real estate investing, a cornerstone of wealth building, involves strategic intelligence and a full grasp of market dynamics. Successful investors adopt diverse techniques to optimize profits and avoid risks in this volatile market.

1. **Long-Term Appreciation**:

Investing for long-term appreciation entails acquiring assets with the assumption that their value would improve over time.

This approach capitalizes on market trends, economic expansion, and development in certain locations. Patience is crucial, as this technique entails hanging onto assets for lengthy periods to gain large appreciation.

Buy and Hold:

- Approach: Acquire properties with the purpose of owning for the long term.

- Execution: Focus on places with consistent appreciation potential and substantial rental demand. Emphasize property management for sustainable financial flow.

- Advantages: Builds long-term wealth, offers a stable income stream, and allows for tax advantages over time.

2. **Rental Income**:

Generating rental revenue is a core approach, when investors acquire buildings with the goal to lease them to tenants.

Consistent cash flow from rent payments can provide a consistent revenue stream and serve as a hedge against market volatility. Location, property management, and market demand play crucial roles in the success of this strategy.

Short-Term Rentals:

- Approach: Invest in homes ideal for short-term rentals through sites like Airbnb.

- Execution: Consider location, local legislation, and property management for best returns. Stay alert to travel trends and local demand.

- Advantages: Higher rental revenue possibilities compared to typical long-term leasing.

3. **Fix-and-Flip**:

The fix-and-flip approach involves acquiring inexpensive or distressed buildings, restoring or improving them, and selling for a profit. This technique involves a good eye for property value and remodeling expenses, paired with effective project management.

Successful execution may generate speedy profits, making it a popular alternative for investors with a desire for hands-on engagement.

- Approach: Purchase dilapidated houses, remodel them, and sell for a profit.

- Execution: Carefully examine remodeling expenses, market demand, and prospective resale value.

Efficient project management is vital to reduce holding costs.

- Advantages: Quick gains, especially in rising markets. It requires a strong eye for property value increase.

4. **Real Estate Investment Trusts (REITs)**:

For individuals wanting a more passive investment, Real Estate Investment Trusts (REITs) offer a way to participate in a diverse portfolio of income-generating properties. REITs give liquidity and the potential to benefit from real estate gain without direct property ownership. Dividends from REIT assets can be a steady income source.

5. **Real Estate Crowd funding**:

In the era of digital banking, real estate crowd financing has gained popularity. This technique includes numerous investors pooling their resources to collectively participate in a real estate project.

Online platforms ease this process, allowing accessibility to a greater group of investors. Crowd funding increases diversification and lowers the barrier to entry for those seeking real estate exposure.

- Approach: Pool funds with other investors to participate in larger real estate projects.

- Execution: Utilize internet platforms to access a broad selection of real estate assets with fewer capital needs.

Research the crowd financing platform's track record and project selection standards.

- Advantages: Offers diversification, decreased risk, and access to institutional-quality projects without the requirement for considerable cash.

6. **Commercial Real Estate Investments**:

Investing in commercial assets, such as office buildings, retail spaces, or industrial complexes, can yield better profits but frequently demands a larger financial commitment. Understanding the local company climate, economic trends, and leasing structures is key in this strategy.

Commercial real estate investments can provide a balance of rental income and opportunity for property appreciation.

7. **Tax Liens and Deeds**:

Some investors pursue the unique approach of obtaining tax liens or deeds. This entails acquiring properties with outstanding tax liabilities and either earning interest on the unpaid taxes or securing title through foreclosure. While this method can be difficult and differs by country, it can provide unique opportunities for individuals well-versed in the legal and regulatory context.

Tax Lien Investing

- Approach: Purchase overdue property tax liens at auctions.

- Execution: Research local tax lien regulations and estimate the risk associated with each case. Gain preference over other liens on the property.

- Advantages: Can result in large profits, and in certain situations, lead to owning the property at a fraction of its market worth.

8. **Risk Mitigation through Portfolio Diversification**:

Diversifying a real estate portfolio over diverse property kinds, regions, and investment techniques is a risk mitigation approach.

By diversifying assets, investors may offset losses in one area with profits in another, producing a more robust and balanced portfolio.

9. **Value Investing**:

- Approach: Identify undervalued properties with solid characteristics.

- Execution: Conduct in-depth market study to discover properties below their inherent worth. Look for distressed homes, motivated sellers, or regions with development prospects.

- Advantages: Potential for considerable capital appreciation when the market acknowledges the property's true value.

10. **Cash Flow Investing**:

- Approach: Prioritize assets that provide regular positive cash flow.

- Execution: Analyze rental revenue, operational expenditures, and debt payment to guarantee a sustainable cash flow. Focus on properties with significant rental demand and potential for rent appreciation.

- Advantages: Provides monthly income, decreasing dependent on property appreciation.

12. **Development Projects**:

- Approach: Invest in real estate development projects for increased profits.

- Execution: Requires a detailed grasp of local zoning rules, building costs, and market demand. Manage risks by collaborating with competent developers and completing careful feasibility studies.

- Advantages: Potential for big profits but includes more risk and a longer investment horizon.

13. **Joint Ventures**:

- Approach: Collaborate with other investors to combine resources and skills.

- Execution: Form alliances with persons who provide complementary talents or financial resources. Clearly clarify roles, duties, and profit-sharing agreements.

- Advantages: Leverage collaborative strengths, share risks, and access possibilities that may be tough individually.

14. **Triple Net Leases**:

- Approach: Invest in buildings where renters cover property bills like as taxes, insurance, and upkeep.

- Execution: Select properties with creditworthy tenants on long-term contracts. Evaluate the stability of the tenant's business.

- Advantages: Provides a regular revenue stream with fewer landlord duties.

Emerging Trends in Estate Management

In analyzing the ever-evolving landscape of estate management, it is obvious that the industry is facing a deep transition defined by dynamic tendencies. These evolving trends not only reflect the evolution of cultural values but also underline the increasing integration of technology and the requirement for sustainability. As we look into the significant themes driving the future of estate management, it becomes evident that adaptation and innovation are important.

One notable trend that cannot be missed is the growing digital revolution of estate management.

The integration of technology such as artificial intelligence, data analytics, and smart building solutions has transformed how properties are maintained. From predictive maintenance and energy efficiency to tenant involvement and security, these technology developments boost operational efficiency and contribute to a more smooth and intelligent administration of properties.

Sustainability has emerged as a non-negotiable focus element in estate management.

With an increased awareness of environmental effect, there is a growing need for eco-friendly and energy-efficient solutions in property construction and management. From green building certifications to the incorporation of renewable energy sources, estate managers are adopting sustainable techniques that not only line with global environmental goals but also appeal with socially aware tenants and investors.

The notion of wellness in real estate is gaining major popularity. Beyond the usual measurements of property worth, focus is increasingly placed on developing environments that improve the physical and emotional well-being of inhabitants.

Estate managers are introducing facilities like as fitness centers, green areas, and wellness programs, understanding the link between a healthy living environment and overall tenant satisfaction.

Furthermore, the advent of remote work has forced a reevaluation of the traditional office space and, subsequently, the management of commercial properties. Flexibility and flexibility are increasingly crucial as estate managers explore novel methods to maximize space consumption and accommodate to the changing demands of a scattered workforce.

In the domain of residential estates, community-centric development is becoming increasingly prominent.

Estate managers are working on establishing lively and inclusive communities by including public areas, communal facilities, and social engagement activities. This tendency represents a change towards understanding the importance of building a sense of belonging and connection among inhabitants.

As estate management continues to grow, regulatory and legal issues increasingly come to the forefront.

Compliance with evolving laws and regulations, particularly in areas such as data privacy and construction rules, is becoming a vital feature of good estate management.

CONCLUSION

In conclusion, "Mastering Real Estate" stands as a complete and helpful reference for anybody wishing to traverse the convoluted environment of real estate with skill and confidence. Throughout its pages, the book has artfully weaved together a tapestry of knowledge, elegantly blending theoretical concepts with practical applications. By digging into the subtleties of property assessment, investment methods, market analysis, and negotiating techniques, the author has presented readers with a well-rounded grasp of the dynamic and ever-evolving world of real estate.

One of the book's significant qualities resides in its ability to appeal to both seasoned experts and those fresh to the industry. The author's clarity of thinking and simple language makes complicated ideas readily consumable, while the inclusion of real-world examples and case studies provides a depth of pragmatism that is crucial for success in the real estate sector.

Furthermore, "Mastering Real Estate" beyond the world of conventional education; it serves as a mentor, helping readers through the complexities of decision-making and risk management.

By highlighting the need of adaptation and foresight, the book educates its audience not only with the essential information but also with the strategic attitude crucial for surviving in the uncertain real estate world.

The book also addresses the ethical elements of real estate negotiations, highlighting the value of honesty and openness in developing enduring professional partnerships. This ethical grounding sets "Mastering Real Estate" distinct, highlighting the need of responsible and sustainable practices in a business that significantly effects communities and economies.

As readers flip the last pages, they are left not simply with a wealth of information but with a renewed sense of strength and preparation. "Mastering Real Estate" transcends being a simply instructional resource; it becomes a valued companion on the way to become a skilled and ethical real estate agent.

In essence, this book acts as a lighthouse for individuals desiring to traverse the nuances of the real estate business with expertise. Whether one is entering on a career in real estate or wanting to develop current talents, the information offered inside these pages will definitely reverberate for years to come.

"Mastering Real Estate" is not simply a book; it is a path to success, a mentor in paper, and a timeless reference for individuals wishing to make their imprint in the ever-evolving environment of real estate.